Bb Trumpet 1

for Mallory
BIGGER THAN THE SKY

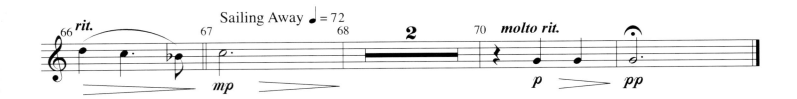

BIGGER THAN THE SKY pg. 2

BIGGER THAN THE SKY pg. 2

F Horn

for Mallory
BIGGER THAN THE SKY

Jon Bubbett
ASCAP

BIGGER THAN THE SKY pg. 2

Trombone

for Mallory
BIGGER THAN THE SKY

Jon Bubbett
ASCAP

BIGGER THAN THE SKY pg. 2

Tuba

for Mallory
BIGGER THAN THE SKY

Jon Bubbett
ASCAP

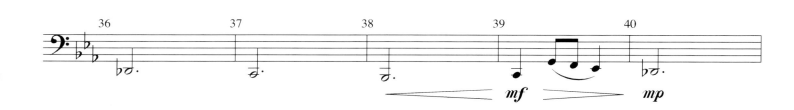

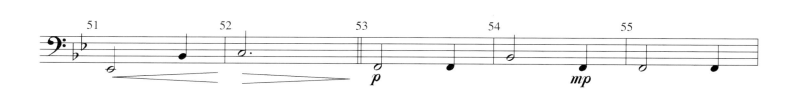

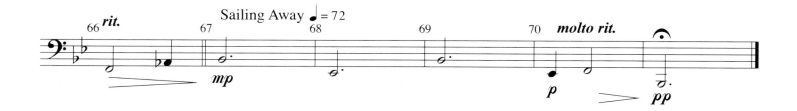

BIGGER THAN THE SKY pg. 2

BIGGER THAN THE SKY

for Mallory

Jon Bubbett
ASCAP

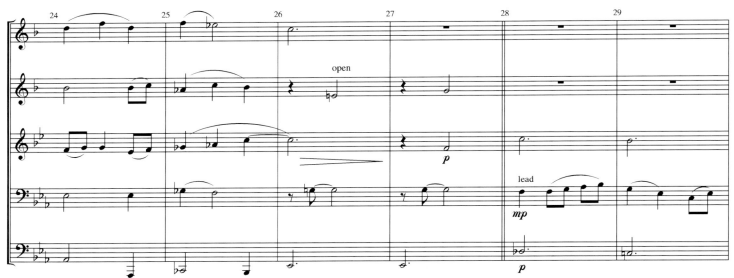

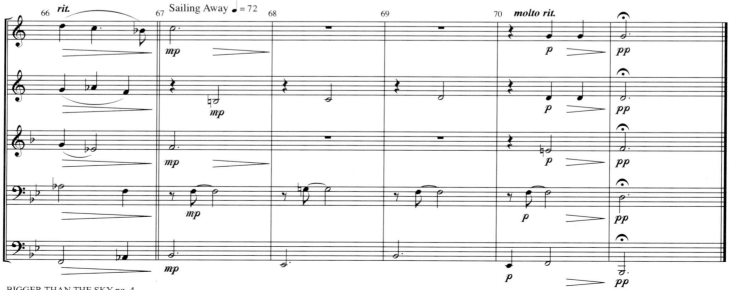